Fancy & Fun: Things to do Over the Age of Maturity

Pamela Brown

COPYRIGHT

Copyright © 2025 Fancy & Fun: Things to do Over the Age of Maturity

by Pamela Brown

Editor: Armor of Hope Writing & Publishing Services, LLC.,

Denise M. Walker

All rights reserved. Except as permitted under the U.S. Copyright Act of 1976, no part of this publication, in whole or in part, may be reproduced, distributed, or transmitted in any form or by any means, including photocopying, recording, or other electronic or mechanical methods without prior written permission from the author.

Dedication

This book is dedicated to all the mature, wise and seasoned women over 50 and still living life, even up to your 90's, or even longer. We are relevant and still living for *FANCY & FUN* things to do.

Special thanks to my daughter Tayler Brown for her artist ability which gave me my book cover as well as my dear friend Shelbie for formulating and putting my book cover in perspective. To my dear Editor thank you for your patient's this has been a long time coming.

Disclaimer

This book is intended for ladies over 50 looking to add more adventure and excitement to your already fulfilling life. Try all these *FANCY & FUN* ideas at your own risk, hopefully resulting in more things for you to experience and have fun with.

Contents

Section One: Love, Family, & Friends 8

Section Two: Beautiful, Fit, & Healthy You *(Over 50 and Loving it)* 16

Section Three: Relaxation.. 33

Section Four: Redefining Yourself 44

Book Summary... 59

About the Author 60

Section One
Love, Family, & Friends

1
Listen to God's voice

Listen to God's voice for clear concise direction. I promise God will never steer you wrong.

2
Know and Love who God is

Once you know and love who God is, if you don't already, you will never be the same.

3
Love Self First

Before you can love someone else, you must take time to love yourself first.

4
Be One with you Family

We are not on this earth alone. Spend time with your family and friends.

5
Keep Meaningful People in your Life

People who can help you grow and inspire you to do and be a better person are truly a gem. Keep them in your treasury.

6
Enjoy Doing Things with your Children & Grandchildren

You only have one life to live. Live surrounded by people you love. Go have fun with your children and grandchildren. Instill wisdom and enjoyable keepsake memories in them.

Take Away

If nothing else, take time to first enjoy you. Then, enjoy your family and friends. Having meaningful people in your life is a fulfillment. Enjoy not being here alone. If you find yourself alone, start being open to the idea of having your family and friends in your life. Stay connected and celebrate your relationships.

Section Two
Beautiful, Fit, & Healthy You
(Over 50 and Loving it)

1

Invest in an Electric Toothbrush

An electric toothbrush with a soft bristle cleans better than a regular toothbrush. Your teeth will thank you.

2
Exfoliate your Skin

Exfoliate dead skin cells at least twice a week. Your skin will have a glow that is simply irresistible. You can find good and inexpensive exfoliates at your local store.

3

Don't Forget about your Face and Neck

Find a good cleansing regimen that works well for you. Use a cleanser, eye cream, serum, and moisturizer. In addition, use a SPF 50 sunscreen to protect your skin.

4

Pamper Yourself

Find a beauty college near you that offers spa-like treatments at discounted rates. Take advantage of the ones for hair, facials, massages, and so much more.

5
Fancy Hairstyles For the Mature Woman

If you find yourself struggling with thinning hair, by all means, get a cute Pixy Cut and look fancy.

6

Do Yourself a Favor, get a Foot Massage

Your feet are a precious commodity; keep living and taking care of your assets. It's called reflexology. Get one.

7
Stretching & Flexibility

Stretching the body before the start of your day is an awesome wake up call for the body. Preparing your muscles and joints for a fantastic day is essential to a healthier and stronger you. Stretching before bedtime is a bonus.

8
Stay Healthy and Active

Ladies, to maintain the independence of your health, you must take control. If you haven't already started doing something for better fitness in your life, it's not too late to start today. Don't stop living. Stay active.

9

Have a Healthy Support System

If you find yourself unable or not motivated to work alone, gather some friends and plan a workout day, or look at a workout video.

10
Keep Moving

Invest in a good pair of walking shoes and move. Look into a dance or step class for stretching, flexibility, and balance. Walk around the house lifting dumbbells. While sitting on the couch or in a chair, do some exercises. Look at some videos, and your body will thank you.

11
Drink Water, your Body Needs it

Water is essential to our body; it needs water like a plant needs it to survive. Without water, your body will surely suffer. Invest in a water bottle, and take it with you when you are out running errands or at work.

12

Treat Yourself to a Healthy Smoothie

Learn how to make a heathy smoothie that's satisfying to your tastebuds, and don't forget to add spinach. After all, you're making a healthy one. Look at your social media for some ideas.

13

Invest in a Juicer

If you're that person that takes in fruit and vegetables at least 20-30 times a week, awesome job. If not, no worries just start now with baby steps. Juicing is a WONDERFUL alternative. Look up juicing videos and get to drinking (juice ladies). Your soul will thank you.

14

Eat a Well-Balanced Diet

Plan out your meals in advance. Incorporate and cook foods you like to eat, and maintain a healthy balance.

15

Eat Fried Foods only Twice a Month

If you must have fried foods, do so in moderation; your heart will thank you.

Take Away

Take care of your skin. Remember, the skin is the largest organ of the body. Keep your skin and face well moisturized. Drink plenty of water. Your body needs it. Water is essential to your body and overall health. Remember, you are truly what you eat. Maintain a well balance diet. Stay fit, and no matter what keep moving. Keep stretching, stay flexible, maintain good balance, and posture.

Section Three
Relaxation

1

Start your day with a prayer and a positive attitude

Set your day up for a calm, successful, and relaxing one. The outcome will be well worth it. Your mind, body, and soul will thank you.

2

Cooking can be as Pleasurable as Relaxing

When you find yourself in the kitchen cooking after a long day, turn on your favorite Jazz tunes or soft piano music, and embrace the aromatics of your meal.

3

Dance, Dance, Dance

Listen, Ladies! Whether it's a praise party or a soulful party, don't go looking for a party. Bring the fun and relaxing party to you. Get your partner or dance by yourself. Most importantly, have fun. Find a space at home and dance.

4

Light a Candle and Listen to Music While Taking a Bath

Soothe the soul and mind with a little relaxion. Enjoy the flickering of the light and smooth sounds of your favorite tunes that shower you with peace. Relax, release, and unwind to a peaceful evening.

5
Learn how to Meditate

Find a quiet space in your environment. Close your eyes, put your mind on pause, and focus on nothing for as long as you can. Concentrate on your breathing and just be one with yourself. Keep practicing. You will get to that place and love it.

6

Make Your Bedroom Stunning

Allow your relaxing space to be inviting, elegant, and beautiful like you. Let your bedroom fit your personality. Place candles and silk flowers with the smell of sweet perfume on your dresser. Next to your bed, on your nightstand, add a small waterfall, and listen to the calm trickling sound of mother nature.

7

Practice on your Partner or Treat Yourself

Invest in a massage table, and practice giving each other a massage, or perform the technique on your bed. If all else fails, go and treat yourself to a relaxing massage.

8

Read A Good Book

Finally, when your day is all said and done and you're ready for bed, turn the TV off, and allow your mind to take you to a place of wonder and excitement. Read a book that inspires your thoughts and mind to relax.

9

Listen to some Relaxing Music

If you should ever find yourself where you just can't sleep, and your brain won't go on pause, turn your electronic device on to the relaxing sounds of therapeutic spa like music, and off to sleep you will go.

Take Away

Listen to your mind, body, and soul. Every now and then, give yourself a treat, the treat of relaxing and allowing yourself to just enjoy you. Find what soothes you, and embrace it throughout your daily activities. Enjoy some quiet time for yourself. Explore what makes you relax and keep it.

Section Four
Redefining Yourself

1

You're never too old to learn new things

Never allow your voice or someone else's to talk you out of learning something new and fun (Go for it).

2
Say what you Mean and Stand by it

Hopefully you've learned by now that you can't make everyone happy, and it's okay. Say what you mean and stand by it. It's okay to say no, even if someone doesn't agree with your decision. **Trust yourself!**

3
Know your Worth and Purpose

Never allow your thoughts to make you think you are not relevant or important. You have so much wisdom and advice to share with the world.

4

Be an Example for Young People

Allow the youth to see what loving each other truly looks like and what it means. Back in the day, it took a village to raise a child. Let's try and keep our children out of the wilderness. Be a positive role model to the youth. Listen to the younger generation, and value their opinions.

5

Don't stop Setting Goals for Yourself

If you can see it, you can do it. Stop talking yourself out of your success no matter the age. Baby steps are allowed. Just keep working toward your goals. Continue exercising your brain power.

6

Be a Minimalist

Learn to let go; keeping clutter will reap wreak havoc on the mind. Less is always best.

7

Level up Your Next Level

Go and be **Fancy,** *Fabulous*, and *Free*. Step up your game to reinvent yourself for a better you; make heads turn.

8

Join a Social or Community Group of people

Get out and meet new people. Go places you've never been before or try things you've never experienced. Have a picnic in the park (start with that). Plan dinner dates or dinner parties with friends.

9
Flirt, Date and Love

You only live once. Flirt with the person you have your eyes set on, as long as it's safe to do. Date your spouse or try meeting new people, fall in love, and enjoy it.

10
Join a Book Club

Enjoy your journey of reading and learning with a group of friends or the opportunity to meet new people.

Learn to Forgive

Be an example to people who you can forgive, but at the same time, teach a person how to treat you. Expect nothing but respect.

Take Away

Look at how far you have come. You are a fancy, mature, and seasoned woman who couldn't made it this far without GOD. Stay relevant and important to yourself. Always know what matters. We are getting older, yet we are still wise and able to teach others the joy of this wonderful stage in our life. So, go out, be *Fancy* and have fun doing it. Love, live, enjoy people, and most importantly love you.

Make it about you. On these next two pages, I want you to explore you. Write down goals and fun things you do or thought about doing, and go do it. This is your journey, your blank canvas. Go have fun, and be fancy doing it.

Blank Canvas

Goals:

Blank Canvas

Goals:

_____
_____
_____
_____
_____
_____
_____
_____
_____
_____
_____
_____
_____
_____

Book Summary

Being a woman over the age of 50 and going through changes at different stages in her life, Pamela Brown needed to know and feel that she was still relevant. After raising a son and still raising her teenage daughter, the author learned that her life was still important, and there was much for her to do. At this stage, she believes women still have a lot of living ahead of them.

In this, her debut book, she shares ideas of how women over 50 can listen to and cater to yourself. You only have one life to live, and she wants to see you enjoy it, remain in good health, peace, find time to relax, and surround yourself with the people you love and care about.

About the Author

As a medical professional, Author Pamela Brown has had the opportunity to see an aging population for many years. This has opened her eyes to respond to her calling of helping others age gracefully.

In addition, coming from a place of teaching exercise classes, in the past, kept her in tune with maintaining fitness goals, as well as good mental health, which is what she hopes, you, her audience will also embrace on your aging gracefully journey.

Finally, her daily searches for moments where she can be thankful and appreciative for, God first, then for her family and friends is also significant.

Overall, Author Pamela Brown looks forward to you, her reader, allowing her to share her tips and come along beside you as she teaches you how to be Fancy and have Fun over 50.

www.ingramcontent.com/pod-product-compliance
Lightning Source LLC
LaVergne TN
LVHW051203080426
835508LV00021B/2775